LIDS

CRACKING YOUR GLASS CEILING

LEAH CHILENGWE

Commissioned Publication

ISBN: 978 0 86071 831 4

All thoughts and opinions in this book are that of the author.

e-mail your questions and comments to the author at:
info@lifewithleah.co.uk

Please Note: Where some Scripture quotations include italics,
these are for the purpose of emphasis by the author.

A Commissioned Publication Printed by

MOORLEYS
Print, Design & Publishing
info@moorleys.co.uk · www.moorleys.co.uk

Dedication

To Susan Henderson: thank you for believing me even when others did not. Thank you for standing strong against injustice even when it wasn't popular, and it cost you friends. Every soldier needs an ally; I couldn't have done this battle without you.

I love you eternally.

Contents

Acknowledgements

To the greatest support squad known to man! My husband Nelson and daughters Kookie and Zo; thank you for encouraging me to keep walking even though you were close to drowning yourselves.
I love you guys.

Introduction

As human beings, we face many challenges in life. Some are easy to overcome, and others are not. The one area where I see people struggle the most is in breaking the limitations imposed upon them by society, family, or self. I call these and many other limitations, 'Lids', in this book. Someone once said, "Abraham Lincoln was born in a log cabin, but he did not stay there, he walked out, and that is what made him the great man that he was. The more you dream in life, the further you get. It is, therefore, our responsibility to be the custodians of the progress we want to see in our lives.

There are no limits to what we can achieve when we are really desperate. Moreover, it is when we believe we reach higher heights that we discover what we are made of. We should never put a cap on anything that we want to see manifest in our lives. The road to the realisation of our goals has many barriers. And the barriers we refuse to confront can become the Lids of our future.

In this journey of life, we must always look to push our limits. No obstacle should ever limit our lives. These should be viewed as opportunities to stretch us and help us grow until we reach the finish line. I once read a quote that resonated well with me. It said, "Stand up to your obstacles and do something about them."

When you do, you will find that those same obstacles do not have half the strength you thought they had. Perseverance and persistence are paramount to achieving your goals in life, regardless of the impossibilities that lie ahead. It is these traits that distinguish the strong from the weak, the overcomer from the defeated.

If you are tired of living a 'contained' life and you want to go beyond, then this book is for you. It is time to smash that glass ceiling! Remember, the ceiling is never a problem when you realise you are the hammer.

1

THOUGHTS AND IMAGINATIONS

"You only gravitate to the level of your most dominant thoughts". When I first read this saying, it challenged me and got me thinking about my life and the experiences I had been through. I asked myself questions: What if the successes in my life were dependent on the level of my thoughts? What was the *mental real* that I was playing to myself? Because of these thoughts and imaginations: was I growing or was I stagnant?

Many are the mountains I have failed to climb; plans and careers I have had to let go, despite how hard I tried and how far I had progressed. Coming up against these mountains has been frustrating. I had dreams I wanted to achieve, places I wanted to go, but at times, however hard I wanted to flap my wings and fly, I always seemed to come up short.

A wise person once told me that who I am, and what I am doing today, is a direct result of all of my past and present thoughts, words, and experiences. It is the accumulation of these dominant thoughts, and experiences, that form what we believe about ourselves.

And in matters of achievement, one can only do what one believes he or she is empowered to do. Let us unpack that for a minute. Whatever you believe to be true is shaped by your past, and your present thoughts, words and experiences that combine to form such a belief system.

Beginnings

Many of our beliefs were instilled in us when we were very young, at a time when we did not really have any say in most matters. If the transmitted beliefs are healthy and productive; we have a winning formula to help us reach our goals and dreams. The converse of this can be disastrous. It is these flawed beliefs that result in unproductive, unhealthy, defeatist attitudes and patterns that may now be limiting factors in our lives.

It is my firm belief also that before anything or anyone can hinder our progress; the first "Lid" we encounter in our lives is ourselves. As human beings, it is easy to default to blaming others outwardly, and/or previous experiences for the issues we face. I believe, however, that the ability to critically and honestly evaluate ourselves is the first step to overcoming the barriers we face.

It is also important to remember that in all the previous experiences we have been through, we too have been contributors to the outcomes of those situations. We must be cognisant of our responsibility to review and critically analyse areas where we could have done better, to grow from those challenges in life. I am not talking about blatant abuse here, but rather, the regular day to day conflicts we face as individuals.

What is a Lid?

Lids are limitations or barriers that are tied to a person's image and what he or she believes is achievable in life. The lower the self-worth, the lower the expectations such a person will have for himself or herself. Until that self-perception improves, and until that person believes they can do more, it is likely they will continue to underperform. The factors that make an individual perform below their capabilities are what I call a 'Lid' or 'glass ceiling'.

These Lids or proverbial glass ceilings then become the progress blockers to our dreams and goals for the future, as they influence what we think, or how we see everything around us.

We need to give some thought to this area. I am sure many of us have a few habits and thought patterns that we would like to change or reverse. Thoughts and words are containers of creative power that shape and determine the heights to which we can rise in life.

Your thoughts, words, and actions determine your present reality. Likewise, they can negatively or positively determine the outcomes of your future realities. To take ownership of your daily thoughts, words and actions, you need to identify and understand their connection and influence on the current circumstances in your life. Only then, can you channel these thoughts in the direction of your goals and dreams.

Run the race

Life is like a race. In the bible, Paul says:

Therefore, since we are surrounded by such a great cloud of witnesses, let us throw off everything that hinders and the sin that so easily entangles. And let us run with perseverance the race marked out for us. Hebrews 12:1.

Athletes operate on a similar principle. They seek to perfect their focus and endurance while preparing to run a race. Discipline is, therefore, necessary for any measure of success that is to be achieved. Every athlete wants to perform their best in competitions, otherwise what would be the point? Besides, discipline makes the difference between those who succeed and those who fail. I have also learned that calming the body and mind, or shall I say the art of relaxation, is vital in preparing to be a good athlete. More importantly, athletes in training must pay attention to their thoughts. Only then can they develop a mind-set that aligns with their dreams and aspirations.

Similarly, if you want to see change in your performance,

your career, and life in general, then you need to make a decision to spend time learning about your unique self and what it is that makes you tick.

Doing this, may just be the key that allows you to explore areas of personal growth and ensure that you shed any negativity you may have carried over time. It also prepares you to be ready for the future intended for you.

But how does it work?

I am learning how my mind works and how I can develop it, and afterwards harmonise these newly acquired mental skills with my goals and dreams. Your thoughts have power. Understanding the extent of this power is important.

For athletes, how they think and feel in a given situation, or about performing a specific activity, determine how effectively they apply themselves.

The athlete's whole body expresses his or her thoughts and feelings. However, the intensity of expression does not originate from the body only, but also from the emotions attached to the athlete's thoughts. Consequently, the body has no choice but to perform according to the thoughts in the athlete's mind.

You will only be comfortable doing what you believe you have the power to do. If you want to raise your level of performance, as corny as this may sound, you will have to raise the ceiling of your comfort zone.

What do you normally spend time thinking about? What

is it that tugs on your heartstrings? These thought patterns become your most dominant thoughts, and they have power and a controlling sense of direction. It is because of this that I am mindful of the fact that you will always gravitate or move in the direction of your most dominant thoughts.

I have been known to be quite vocal, in some quarters, something I can neither accept nor deny being true. My husband often says he 'thinks' for the family, and that I 'speak' for it. I suppose that's ok as some people think before they speak while others seem to speak before they think. However, both camps must remember this: "Whatever you spend time thinking about, you will move towards".

Some years ago, we challenged ourselves to change the way we spoke in our home, focusing on changing our speech from negative to positive. My husband set us all a challenge, to complete every statement coming out of our mouths with the words, "and that's the way I like it!" For example, one of the girls would say, "nobody likes me at school." My husband would then ask: "And that's the way you like it?" This change was at first met with resistance, but with time, it helped us all to take stock of our words and to check the thoughts that ran riot in our minds.

Everyone started to see positive changes in their own sphere of life. The good news is this; it worked, and still is working for every member of our family, as we continue to understand that our words have power. The bible says in Proverbs 18:21:

Death and life are in the power of the tongue, and those

who love it will eat its fruits.

When you become aware of the Lids formed by thoughts and imaginations in your life, you must rebuke and eliminate/suppress those that are simply not in line with God's thoughts, or those that do not line up with your goals and dreams. We must learn to dwell on the things we want to accomplish and how we plan to do so. Then by principle, you will eventually gravitate towards the positive thoughts, and your words and actions will align with the goals God set for you, until they become realities in your life.

When you become more aware of how limiting or liberating your thoughts can be, you will, without doubt, be careful with your thoughts, and consequently the words from your mouth.

See it/Achieve it

So, since we now know that our mind creates pictures from our thoughts and words, we need to train the mind to focus on the mental images of the things we want to see manifest in our lives.

Mahatma Gandhi once said *"men often become what they believe themselves to be. If I believe I cannot do something, it makes me incapable of doing it. But when I believe I can, then I acquire the ability to do it even If I didn't have it in the beginning."*

The idea that what we repeatedly think about, and how we think about it, will eventually become a reality, is not a nebulous concept, it is a direct reflection of our thoughts and actions.

The main thought I would like for us to take from this chapter is this: As we journey through the rest of the book, the foremost thing we must remember is that the first potential Lid you will encounter in life is yourself.

Our dominant thoughts shape our lives, our beliefs and also direct our actions and consequently what we become. So basically, the principle is that thought and actions are the stepping stones to achievement.

I use various examples in this book to highlight the common Lids we will potentially encounter in life. It is critical to remember in all the examples; I too, could have at one time or another been a Lid to someone else. In every challenging situation, no one is perfect, as to do so is to give yourself victim status. This label will not only stunt our personal growth but also block progression to all that life has set out for us.

Proverbs 23:7 New King James Version (NKJV):
For as he thinks in his heart, so is he. "Eat and drink!" he says to you, but his heart is not with you.

Notice how we think governs who we are. Solomon here shows that a man can say, "eat and drink" and yet he is not really friendly and hospitable, as his words would imply, but his heart grudges every crumb he gives you.

"Discipline makes the difference between those who succeed and those who don't.

NOTES:

What thoughts can you identify about yourself that are stopping you from progressing in different areas of your life?

2

BREAK SOME!

We were all created to achieve the absolute best in life, at whatever level that may be. This is the reason why we should evolve and strive for what we consider to be the absolute best for our lives.

There are many hoops, however, that we must jump through to reach our God-given destiny. This is because society conditions us to conform to pre-set rules and systems that we often do not even understand.

"Play the game," they say, *"suck it up a little, lose yourself; that's the only way to get ahead..."*

This sounds sensible to some extent, I guess. However, after critical analysis, one may be forgiven for thinking this is a "behave as I want you to behave and in return, I will reward you." This is control and because it is, this behaviour is counterintuitive to personal or corporate growth.

Toe the line

In my experience, the belief that we must lose ourselves to progress, has mostly felt like "the more you toe the line"; it did not matter what that line may have been at the time, "the better the opportunities you seemed to get."

"But that is common sense Leah," I hear you say. True, but is it not also our job to 'inspect the line' before toeing it? We all have a responsibility for ourselves as well as the community we live in, to ensure that we are walking in truth and integrity. We must all make it a point not to lose ourselves for the sake of trying to get ahead in life. That is why we must ensure that our primary focus is being led by the voice of God.

Maybe this was my problem, and perhaps the reason why when it came to my own progress, I often mostly found myself in 'accidental promotions'; I was never good at keeping silent, when I felt that things needed to be highlighted for improvement! I believe that being in an environment that values you as a person, and consequently your voice, is imperative to your growth.

This "sucking up" culture is set by leaders whose aim is to ensure that their subordinates are controlled to a point where they totally lose their courage to speak up. These leaders exist in environments that do not pose a real challenge to their leadership, therefore making it difficult for them to receive feedback they deem as negative. This kind of "set up" is what I call dysfunctional leadership; a setting where service to self is more important than the greater good of the community.

That said, not everyone who is a leader is dysfunctional. I have come across some brilliant people across the span of humanity. However, the few, who think that they are 'supreme' leaders, tend to have a knee-jerk reaction to any perceived challenge to their authority because they are so used to hearing..."yes boss"! Remember the saying, "absolute power corrupts absolutely"? There it is!

It is in such environments that we tend to have rules that have Lid-like tendencies, deliberately set that way, to control and hinder the progress of the people within them. Lid like principles will impact negatively on the people and the overall culture of the institution.

Just for you

My experience, in some institutions, is that rules are made but only for the benefit of a specific group. This is called "exclusion". And then there are those rules that are created to 'contain others.' This is called "oppression."

I know organisations and/or communities that work in this way. And sadly, I discovered the same thing in the church.

In certain communities, several people may be forgiven

for believing that they have a greater chance at success if they turned a blind eye to the issues that were blatantly concerning to them. For me, I have never had an issue with honouring leadership and following cultural norms. I, however, have also felt strongly that it is unhealthy if raising concerns in any community is perceived as an attack and even problematic by the leadership. This is what is called gagging. A gag is a Lid, it stifles your voice and eventually stunts your growth.

It is saddening when you encounter this in any community. Some leaders' desire is for people to switch off their own minds, ignore the evidence, and blindly follow them. This is most common in churches, as it is easy to use a higher power as backing to introduce a set of cultural norms that are probably man made.

When we blindly adopt a set of principles, we become automatons. As humans, it is important to speak up over issues that bring us discomfort. This action will take courage, to not blindly overlook uneasiness, but in seeing it, and conquering it.

It is important to note that in any group of diverse people it is impossible for everyone to see things in the same way. Fair mindedness should be paramount in every leader's mind when building an environment where people are called to grow. When rules and opportunities only favour a certain group of people, it destroys the people who don't benefit.

God loves diversity, and this is the reason why he made us all different in shape, colour, size, gifts, and temperament. To honour or follow a leader blindly because of a culture that favours those who do not question the status quo is dangerous.

When my children were younger, their usual response to every command or suggestion was "why?" This drove me crazy, just like many other parents out there. But I am no different to what my children were. I am an inquisitive and challenging person, but my actions come from a good place, a desire to pursue what I consider to be right, except it has resulted in me "falling on my own sword", sometimes.

Who made these rules anyway?

I learnt an important lesson on my journey to self-discovery. The lesson was simple: Before I conform to any set of rules, I should ask who it is that made them in the first place.

The next question should be: And why those rules in particular? As I said earlier, I am all for boundaries, but I am also fully aware that some of these rules are implemented to stop individuals and sometimes, whole communities, from progressing by creating uniformity, which consequently hinders diversity and individuality.

Sometimes, one person or a small group sets the "standards" to which others are expected to conform in that community. How the leader of a group or a society looks, thinks, walks and talks become the mould that "everyone else" must fit in.

I understand the importance of rules. I believe rules must be obeyed for legal purposes, accountability, consistency in decision making, promotion of trust and fairness, and to get things done.

But does it?

I have been in different scenarios where I tried, as best as I could, to tick the boxes, to submit to leadership, so to speak. But what does submission to rules and/or leadership mean? Does it mean unquestioningly following a person or an institution's way of doing things?

I have come across many people who unquestioningly follow a leader in the name of honour. How can one consider this acceptable? If honour means blindly following a leader, then by deduction we may as well say that Hitler's followers were right in executing his orders. We must ask ourselves this question: is this the way we are called to operate? And as leaders: is this the kind of honour we desire from the people we lead?

To clap for people we believe have the power to open the doors we desire is destructive. This behaviour says, "I will do anything in order to please you so I can get something in return." Honour, however, elevates and celebrates, but also speaks up, to help the leader do better and to keep improving at what he or she does.

I find it easy to speak up against any form of injustice. This is because I have always believed that I was given a voice to speak into people's lives and the issues that affect us as humans. Most people do not appreciate this side of me, and it has often landed me into trouble.

I have been ostracised and sometimes marginalised because of the desire of some leaders to shape me into an image they wanted of me. The thing is this, only God has the right to mould us into what He chooses for us to be. We read in Isaiah 64:8, (NIV):

"Yet you O Lord are our father, we are the clay and you are the potter, we are all the work of your hand."

I am well aware of the importance of leaders in our lives, after all. And as I said earlier, I am a mentor and a leader of many, myself. What we cannot do as leaders, however, is gag the people in our care under the guise of a required respect for our leadership. We must remember that God has given us, His people, a free will and choice. God gave us this because He loves us, and He knows that allowing us freedom gives us room to grow. Our role, as leaders, is to simply guide and encourage them to be the best of who God designed them to be.

From experience I believe it is common sense to allow people to "outwork" their purpose, mistakes, and all. I have come across leaders who "write people off" because the individual did not take the advice that they had given. A leader who feels insecure because the people under his care are not doing everything as they are told must check whether he or she is 'leading' or 'controlling'.

Control is about ego. It is what leaders do to feel like they are the centre of their universe. However, ultimately, all they want is to take credit for people's progress, replacing God the potter. A good leader strives for influence rather than control.

Am I my brother's keeper?

We live in a world where we are increasingly empowered to speak up especially with the increasing social media platforms available to us. Whether we use that power wisely is a topic for another day.

When you speak up, it is disappointing at times to look around and see people in your world who know the truth of which you speak, but avoid speaking up or at the very least reach out for fear of upsetting the controlling leader.

We were meant to be interdependent as human beings, and we reap what we sow, in one way or another. So, instead of being over-protective of what is ours, we must care enough to stand up for what is right and benefits the people around us.

If I was making a choice to either stand up for truth at the detriment of my position or turning the other way, I know on which side of the truth I would be standing. Do you?

How are you doing?

Writing this book has helped me to assess myself and the different leadership roles I hold. My greatest honour in life is being a mother to two gorgeous girls. As a parent, however, it has been hard to watch my children make their own choices and consequently, their own mistakes. I know I made a fair few when I was younger and still do, I guess. The funny thing is this, though, I have an inert desire to overprotect them, to ensure that they get things right, the first time.

My expectation for them has been that they get good grades, choose the right friends, have the best career, and the list is endless. But in the last few years, I began to question myself whether my desire, which is not wrong in itself, I might add, was for their benefit or mine. What was the motive behind this desire for my children to meet such high expectations?

If I am honest with myself, some of these expectations were about me, about what made me comfortable and happy. I also accept that this desire to ensure that my girls were what I considered "high achievers" was driven by fear. It was the fear of not wanting them to try something five or six times before they get it right.

Of course, I know this is not good, and I am desperately trying to work on it because it is not helpful to my girls. As part of growing up, they will have to make a lot of mistakes to know their limits. They will also need to become comfortable with uncertainty and to understand that failure is not final.

My parenting issues are no different from the challenges most leaders face. Like me, they have standards that must be strictly followed, without question. But I tend to wonder, where is the growth in this? Are we dealing with robots or human beings?

Moreover, controlling leaders must realise that we cannot replace God in the lives of the people under our care. We can advise, care and nurture what is inside the individual; however, we must draw a line in terms of taking away the 'God instances' meant for their personal development.

It is important to remember that the people we lead are not our children. These are people with families and their own responsibilities in their worlds. To discard, or "cancel" an individual because they did not follow your guidance is counterproductive to the mission of growing the very people we were called to lead.

Love is patient and kind. Love is not jealous or boastful or proud or rude. It does not demand its own way. It is not irritable, and it keeps no record of being wronged. It does not rejoice about injustice but rejoices whenever the truth wins out. Love never gives up, never loses faith, is always hopeful, and endures through every circumstance. 1 Corinthians 13: 4-7, (NIV).

The passage above talks about love being patient, kind and never giving up. I read this and it dawned on me, a leader who loves his or her subordinates would not discard them for not following his or her advice because love is what binds us together.

In terms of my girls, it does not matter how many times I tell them to do something, I am available with open arms, regardless of the choices they make.

We must let the people we lead challenge our set benchmarks; otherwise sooner or later the house will burn down! Allow them the freedom to be who they are, to speak freely in a community. And remember, apart from God's, all other rules are subject to change. So, break some and learn something from that if you must!

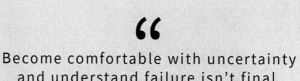

Become comfortable with uncertainty
and understand failure isn't final.

NOTES:

What rules do you think have been barriers to your goals? Do you think these rules are fair and consistent across the board or are these just tailored to slow you down?

3

THE LID OF SILENCE

There is a guy called David in the bible who killed a giant named Goliath. David was the youngest of eight brothers and split his time between the palace and the pasture. Everyone thought he was just a shepherd boy; they judged him by his service to his family and the community rather than by who God said he was.

1 Samuel 16 :10-13, (NIV) outlines how God selects David to be the next king:

Jesse had seven of his sons pass before Samuel, but

Samuel said to him, "The Lord has not chosen these." So, he asked Jesse, "Are these all the sons you have?" "There is still the youngest," Jesse answered. "He is tending the sheep." Samuel said, "Send for him; we will not sit down until he arrives." So, he sent for him and had him brought in. He was glowing with health and had a fine appearance and handsome features. Then the Lord said, "Rise and anoint him; this is the one." So, Samuel took the horn of oil and anointed him in the presence of his brothers, and from that day on the Spirit of the Lord came powerfully upon David.

David had been anointed King by Samuel long before there was a King in David, even while he was still a shepherd boy. And yet because everybody around David knew his background, they considered him unqualified to fight Israel's enemies.

Later in *1 Samuel 17:32-37, (NET)* we see David fight and defeat a giant:

David said to Saul, "Don't let anyone be discouraged. Your servant will go and fight this Philistine!" But Saul replied to David, "You aren't able to go against this Philistine and fight him! You're just a boy! He has been a warrior from his youth!" David replied to Saul, "Your servant has been a shepherd for his father's flock. Whenever a lion or bear would come and carry off a sheep from the flock, I would go out after it, strike it down, and rescue the sheep from its mouth. If it rose up against me, I would grab it by its jaw, strike it, and kill it. Your servant has struck down both the lion and the bear. This uncircumcised Philistine will be just like one of them. For he has defied the armies of the living God!"

David went on to say, "The Lord who delivered me from the lion and the bear will also deliver me from the hand of this Philistine!" Then Saul said to David, "Go! The Lord will be with you."

David had confidence in what he was able to do. He spoke boldly against Goliath. When others referred to Goliath as, "this man", David called him, "this uncircumcised Philistine". When the men of Israel said, "surely he has come up to defy Israel". David said, "...that he should defy the armies of the living God."

The only way David was able to come against Goliath was to rise above his current situation. He had to overcome his self-image as a shepherd boy and see the giant slayer in himself before he could ever do it. David was not just confident in his abilities; he applied his thoughts to God's ability and thus cracked open, the Lid of intimidation and oppression.

Faith always deals with the unseen. To have faith in something - a dream, a plan and a goal, you have to see it in your thoughts first before you can see its manifestation. You do not need someone else to endorse what you already know God has deposited inside of you. David knew in his heart that he was born to rule; therefore, he did not let what the masses thought of him, stop him doing so. I have learnt that at times it is the voices from those around us that can slow down our progression into all we were designed to be.

I left university over twenty years ago and counting. I am now a grown woman, married with grown children, but I realise some people still want to relate to me from the view of their last encounter with me.

It is these types of interactions that can put a cap on where we ought to be. Because we think, well, I have known these people for a very long time; therefore, there may still be truth in what they are saying about me.

Becoming

As we progress through life, it is important to not let other people's opinions of us become the limiting factor to "becoming". It is funny how one negative opinion of us can cripple us and make us forget everything else we have going in our lives. I have learnt to be honest in the way I assess my progress in life as I chip away at the person that I want to become.

You have to ask this very important question: if you ran into you on the street, would you get along with yourself? You have to harness the ability to disagree when what people say about you does not resonate with who you are called to be. We must have the courage to say, "No, I am not who you think I am".

Unfortunately, we are living in a world which is slowly being conditioned to believe that if we disagree with each other, then we cannot have a relationship. It is over and we can never be in the same space again.

To me, this does not make any sense. Aren't disagreements essential to how we socially develop as humans? Isn't a good debate vital to deepening relationships? I can disagree on projects with a colleague at work and still be able to go back and be civil as we continue to work together on other issues. Not so common in some churches. Some are filled with folk who are afraid to challenge the leadership, leading to a culture of silence because of the fear of being ostracised.

I am learning that disagreements are not about going around trying to cause trouble. The issue I find is as long as you articulate your truth, somebody somewhere will become your enemy whether you like it or not. Just because you disagree with someone or something does not mean you should wish for something bad to happen on either of the two.

I have learnt that doing what is right is often hard. When I stood up to church leadership with what they considered "unmitigated gall"; when I said, "No, this is not right," all hell broke loose. When I humbly reflect on what I stood up against, I realise I am not responsible for how it was received. Moreover, I have given up trying to change the distorted picture of me that those who were offended had created.

So, don't stop speaking, be kind to yourself by being a friend to what is right. Don't forget, posterity is watching and will one day hold you accountable.

I have confronted the giants in my life, and I can say with certainty that I have not been the same person after every encounter. Everything changes when you dare to stand up to Goliath and say, "Who are you uncircumcised Philistine?" And some people stand with you while others distance themselves, why? Because they are tied to the giant you stood up against. You have to make peace with that fact.

When I was persecuted out of a church that had been my

spiritual home, after telling the leaders about the pain some of their actions were causing people, I learned a valuable lesson which I later passed on to my girls, and it was this: Never expect everyone to support you when you stand up for the truth. They have their reasons for staying silent, and you have to respect that.

For most people, the conflict between walking in integrity and being considered a betrayer is often hard to reconcile. Even Martin Luther King faced this conflict. Most of the people who did not march with him felt the pain of racial segregation, but they feared the backlash more than they did standing up for the truth.

But you have to understand this truth and *"breathe."* Give people the space to discover that consequences...come to get you, whether you toe the line or not. This is especially when the system is deliberately designed to "cap" the people who stand for what they believe to be true.

There comes a point in your life where you begin to realise what is important. I would rather be labelled difficult or rebellious, than to look in the mirror and not want to look at the 'sister' looking back at me.

David refused to be intimidated by the forces that seemed stronger than him. Not everyone was for him when he said he could take on Goliath, but he refused to back down.

Remember, Eliab, his oldest brother had said to him:

"Why have you come down? And with whom have you left those few sheep in the wilderness?" 1 Samuel 17:28.

Eliab was insinuating that David was arrogant to think that he of all people could confront a giant that had sent a cold chill of fear in the whole army of Israel, for weeks. "Who do you think you are"? This is what was going on in Eliab's mind when he asked David about the "few sheep in the wilderness". But David was not fazed by his older brother's tone of voice and attitude.

We need to get to the point where we do not only change the appearance of the issues we face, but the story too. I do not want to wreck the future of the younger generation by the dysfunctional behaviours that I tolerated in my time.

How unfortunate it is that some people make sure you do not excel in your ground-breaking pursuits because they have the idea that that ground is theirs.

During my church drama, some people said to me, "just be quiet and allow the persecution to pass; the focus will shift to the next drama." This statement itself was problematic but I don't have the time to unpack it. For me, however, no matter how hard I tried, I could not let go of what is in my DNA, which is that I am a *warrior* for justice. We relinquish power to our "Lids" when we fail to speak up under the false impression that things will be different for us. We do this to ourselves because we want to be in good favour but what is favour without integrity?

Silence can cost lives, jobs, families, and even whole communities. It is for this reason that I have always refused to turn a blind eye to acts of injustice. Just because it's not happening to you doesn't make you less responsible for speaking up.

> "
> We must have the courage to say,
> "No, I am not who you think I am".

NOTES:

Which people in your life have the power to speak up for you but don't? Why do you think they refuse to speak up for you?

4

IMMOBILISED BY FEAR

Whenever you raise your voice on issues that affect you personally, some people will call you strident because for them, hearing what you have to say is uncomfortable.

Such perceptions can limit your personal development and potential because it is safer to remain where you are than to rock the boat. The fear of upsetting the apple cart, so to speak, is what stops some people from grabbing all that is meant to be theirs.

I am aware that we are all different in the way we handle life's challenges. Some people may face the same setbacks as you but not struggle at all. There is no one blueprint on how we as people approach the challenges in our lives. The common thread I have found, that gives energy to our struggle, is the confusion attached to any particular challenge.

This tension is fueled by disappointment. We feel disappointed when things do not go the way we expected they would. This disappointment can be with ourselves, our leaders or even just the situation. Leaving disappointment to fester in our souls can lead to discouragement, that is why dialogue is important. To be in an environment that makes you fearful to speak up is a distraction from who you were intended to be, speak up if you must and stand up to the spirit of intimidation.

Again, I think of David, in the bible, he looked at Goliath and thought "I can take him on!" When we read this story in 1 Samuel 17, with the benefit of hindsight, we can easily assume that David was fearless. But I put it to you that this may not have been the case.

The bible says, *"All of the Israelite army was dreadfully afraid"*. There was not one man among them who would take on the Philistine giant. Every one of them fled when Goliath came out. This background information paints a picture of the atmosphere that the Israelites and consequently David was in, at the time of Goliath's taunts. See how easy it is to abort a God-ordained destiny or purpose when you are intimidated by what you choose to magnify.

However, despite all the threats from Goliath, the bible tells us:

David asked the men who were standing with him, "What will be done for the man who kills this Philistine and removes this disgrace from Israel? Just who is this uncircumcised Philistine that he should defy the armies of the living God?"1 Samuel 17:26, (NIV).

How was David able to overcome such a challenging atmosphere? I think that what David saw in front of him, and what he heard coming from Goliath, were nothing compared to what he knew he was carrying inside.

We too can be like David and remember what it is we carry inside whenever we face difficult circumstances. In these situations, we have to focus our sight on a hope that is greater than the challenge we face before us. David did that and he knocked Goliath's head.

It is easy to let fear disqualify us from our God-given purpose, and instead keep us imprisoned in a box of other people's idea of who we ought to be.

Nelson Mandela once said, *"Courage is not the absence of fear, but the triumph over it."* He was right. A brave man is not one who does not feel afraid; it is the one who conquers fear. You too can be brave.

It's not as large as it looks

We were all created to leave a footprint on the earth. I for one want my great great grandbabies to know I existed. But how is this possible if we live our lives through other people's limitations of us and not on a limitless God, who has expectations for us beyond our wildest dreams. If I was a betting woman, I know where my bet would be.

Fear can stifle your potential to leave this planet a better place than you found it. To overcome fear, your desire to achieve must be stronger than the giant that you face. When you fail to do this, you have well and truly stunted your growth.

Learn to go with the discomfort that often precedes the birth of a new day. There is always a price to pay to move into your destiny. And I believe that everything we do, and the people we cross paths with, are all part of our destiny. Nothing happens by chance.

Take Mary, the mother of Jesus, for example, she knew she was carrying the creator of the universe. In case you are a non-Christian reading this, I accept this may blow your mind; however, Mary had to endure the discomfort of a donkey ride before she could get to the place of Jesus' birth.

I was part of my previous church for the best part of 18 years. It was a community I chose, with folk I believed accepted people like me. 18 years is a long time! I believe this emphasises the loyalty and commitment I had to the place. No one turns up to Sunday services, midweek meetings and conferences for that length of time to not be loyal to the community they belong to.

And I had a strong sense, during my time in this establishment, that I was called to lead; that I had a voice, and that God had put me in that place, to thrive. But on reflection, I realise there were deliberate hurdles that were designed to hinder progress for people like me. We had to work twice as hard, to prove our worth, compared to the people who were like the leaders! If it was not a course you had to attend, it was some form of leadership training or the other.

I will never forget my early years in this church. I remember being in service one Sunday when the pastor announced, during his preach, that for all congregants who were 30 years and above; it was time for them to sit down and wait for leadership from the next generation!

I was 30 at the time. THIRTY? Are you kidding me? Was this guy trying to silence me already? I look back now and see a Lid principle at work. This leader was domesticating us when God still had more frontiers for us to conquer. If you are out there and still breathing, God still wants to use you. I remember whispering to a friend at the time, *"that's not what God has for us."* What is funny; the leader in question is in his sixties now. But I guess the time he told us to sit down, in our thirties, God had made an exception for him.

It took a long time before I could decide whether to include this experience in this book or not. But again, eighteen years is a long time! Memories cannot easily be erased just like that because one is fearful of certain people and their cronies, and how they would react to me telling my story. My reasoning is simple: You can account for what you say but not how people choose to react to it.

Besides, my aim in this book is not to accuse but rather to teach. To me, whether a discussion is emotive or not, a good leader always strives to make the best of it. Unfortunately for the church, it has an unhealthy culture of masking Christianese behind certain behaviours that are inexcusable. And in case you were wondering...No, I am not backslidden, no, this is not a demon...and no, it is not a spiritual attack. It is just one family member saying hey, we can do better!

To honour or not to honour

This book is my second publication. My debut publication, "All Grown Up" is available on Amazon, Audible and Kindle. Shameless plug! The book got me into trouble.

One person got their nose out of joint because I had published the book without their blessing and support. So, my girls and I found ourselves facing the greatest giant in our lives. Now, I was born in Zambia, while the offended person was born on another continent far from mine, and from a different race too. My maiden publication was all about my life's challenges, as a woman of colour. I am unclear why this leader would feel upset with me narrating my story.

If my book were about theological matters, I would understand, because it would be disrespectful, I suppose, to assume I was theologically superior to publish a book without the help of this person who would have been deemed theologically superior. Anyway, it has since dawned on me that whoever sets the culture rules the community. It was his community, his culture; his people (although I would beg to differ on this one and say they are God's people).

However, this unhealthy mind-set has unfortunately, become so prevalent in some churches. People have been conditioned to think that one cannot walk in their calling from God, without a pastor's approval. I became, and I still am uncomfortable with this line of reasoning, that says I need to ask for someone's opinion/permission, even when I have heard God tell me to step out. I am not encouraging people to rebel against any church or those in positions of authority, I am only advocating for people to function in God's calling for their lives.

In my case, for example, I thought that writing my first book would be celebrated, but it was not. My family and I were hurried out of the church instead. But it is about time we stopped placing man's knowledge above God's. Being a leader myself, I can confidently say we are just shepherds, but we need to stop just saying it and start acting like it.

When the people we lead start to focus too much on us and not on God, it is our responsibility to redirect their attention back to Him.

Hopefully, this will not be mistaken for dishonour; I am simply putting a voice to the struggle of so many people sitting in the pews today.

I am reminded of Benjamin Franklin's famous quote: *"Without freedom of thought there can be no such thing as wisdom and no such thing as public liberty without freedom of speech."* Need I say more?

Cover versus Lid

Individuals, circumstances, and even whole communities can at times intimidate us so much that we end up imprisoning ourselves from within.

Don't give up on who you are just because of what some people think of you. The blessing is not in what they think or say about you but in who you are; and therein is your victory.

Remember, the same way David slew Goliath and eventually became king, you too have what it takes to bring down your giant. Just lay aside all your fears, and you will be able to see all the limitless possibilities that lie in front of you.

A leader who is a 'covering', nurtures the gift in you and cheers you on, every step of the way until you reach your goal. A covering leader also encourages you to make independent decisions and to believe that you can reach the pinnacle of your gifting even if you make mistakes. A covering leader's love is unconditional, and he or she speaks well of you even when you are not functioning at your best. Furthermore, a covering leader celebrates you even if what you are doing threatens to surpass his or her achievements.

A 'Lid leader', on the other hand, is a container that limits your growth. Such leaders ensure that you do not succeed where they have failed. 'Lid leaders' also challenge what you hear from God and will terminate the relationship when they feel that you are not taking on board what they supposedly heard from God on your behalf.

As I was organising my thoughts for this book, I found my journal from 2004. In it, I had clearly stated that God had given me a word that I would one day write a book in which my story would free others. This was more than sixteen years ago, and It slowly dawned on me, yikes, my book was in a 'container" for all these years!!

Incidentally, during the tough time of my first book incident, I told the leader I keep talking about in this current book, that God had told me to finally leave the church. His reply was, *"you cannot say that, there are plenty of people in mental asylums saying they heard from God."*

I remember this remark as I smile because respectfully, sir, there are plenty of people who are not in mental asylums, preaching to us every Sunday, telling us they heard from God.

This type of leadership is a container that is driven by fear and control; a label that advertises what is not in the can. Is it not funny how some leaders want to control people and yet the Creator of the universe encourages free will? And how He trusts that his Word is patient enough to effect change in people's lives?

"Blessed are those who sit on a pin…"

I was on a bus in Zambia, some years ago, when I saw a sticker with the quote *"Blessed are those who sit on a pin."* Actually, the full statement was: "Blessed are those who sit on a pin, for they shall surely rise."

In a nutshell, if you sit on a pin and complain without standing up, then it isn't painful enough!

Now, I am not one to condone the misuse of scripture-related sayings, but I think that this one spoke volumes, especially for people who complain about toxic leaders or organisations, but do not want to leave or to voice their grievances. What such people need to understand is this; it is unlikely that a toxic leader is going to change their ways unless they are forced to, and even then, those negative traits are typically ingrained in their personality.

So, when it comes to serving under toxic leadership or an organisation, the only wrong move is to do nothing. It empowers that leader or the organisation to continue hurting people. You have options, you have worth. But as I said earlier, if the situation feels painful, yet you are not willing to move, then it is not painful enough......YET! I think that it is important to note that more often than not, people do not leave church, they quit toxic church cultures.

So, do not let fear paralyse you, stand up and do what is right for you and yours.

A brave man is not one who does not feel afraid; it is the one who conquers fear.

NOTES:

What are the fears that are stopping you from stepping out into your goals?

5

THE EMPEROR HAS NO CLOTHES

One of the great works of 19th-century literature is a fairy-tale entitled, the "Emperor's New Clothes", penned by the Danish writer, Hans Christian Andersen.

The story is about two weavers who are contracted by a vain and egotistical emperor to make him the finest and most luxurious set of clothes in the whole empire.

The emperor specifies that the clothes must ooze elegance in keeping with his supreme status. Thus, the two weavers promise the emperor a set of clothes so exquisite that only those who are noble and good people will be able to see it, while the stupid and worthless will not.

But the two weavers, who are not even weavers but swindlers, had heard of the Emperor's vanity and consequently decided to take his failings to their advantage, by pretending to make a set of clothes.

On the day of the parade, the vain emperor fails to admit that he cannot see the clothes for fear that his subjects would think of him as stupid and thus not fit for office.

His ministers also cannot see the clothes, but they still pretend they can, for fear that the people will think they are worthless too.

Finally, a child cries out, "But the Emperor has no clothes. He isn't wearing anything at all!"

Thinking about this story made me realise how in life, we make a variety of choices that either add or take away from us, especially when we are hesitant to voice out our opinions or make our desires known in a given situation.

At times, going with the flow may seem like the easy option, as it minimises the chances of a conflict. In such circumstances, we tend to applaud, affirm, and encourage people even when we know that we do not agree with what they are doing or what they stand for.

I have observed this type of behaviour mostly in people who interact with leaders or individuals they perceive too powerful to mess with by taking a different stand.

So, this is what we say: *"I will clap for you, say you are awesome and amazing; I will tell you what you want to hear, in spite of what I know, because I am fearful of what I may lose if I were honest about my perception of you."*

However, letting people walk all over us takes away from our authentic self. I am also not suggesting being candid for the sake of it. Good relationships call for maturity; at the same time, baseless adulation can be detrimental not only to you but to the receiver of the adulations as well.

An adage I read somewhere went something like this: "I trust your approval because I have received your criticism." What a powerful statement! In a nutshell, it is our responsibility to recognise that not every "check" we encounter in life is an attack; it is not the devil either, but it could be a gift to shape our character.

I cannot emphasise enough how toxic being dishonest is and can be. And lies? In my opinion, these are general statements that one knows to be false or whose intent is to deceive another. It is this last element - the intent to deceive - that distinguishes a common false statement from a plain old lie.

People are telling these lies all the time about others and to some leaders without deep thought of what damage these mistruths do to the person they are lying about.

But am I naked?

Living in a world where we are surrounded by people who only champion an egoistic perspective of life can make us numb to the truth, thus making us lose out on some positive life experiences. This kind of behaviour not only saps our energy but also causes a great deal of stress, because, with time, we learn to default to self-preservation mode, to protect, "my side of the story".

Consequently, we become the first victims of our own lies because we have to believe them first before we can convince others to do so. Dishonesty is always the result of avoiding confrontation at some level. The inevitable result of this kind of behaviour often is lying accompanied by its twin sisters, secrets, and denial. Healing from lying to others requires that we stop deceiving ourselves first.

For change to happen, one must, first of all, know the truth. We cannot change a personality flaw in our lives if we are not aware it exists. Also, how can the people around you change, without you being candid with them? We often hide the painful truth from the person who needs to hear it the most, because we are afraid of how he or she will react, just like what happened to the vain emperor in the opening paragraphs of this chapter.

For those of us in positions of leadership, we often battle the deep-seated fear of getting rejected or losing control of the people in our care. In doing so, we deny such people the freedom to reject our style of leadership or to express their disappointment with us. We, moreover, go to great lengths to protect ourselves from any fallout that may result from having the light of truth directed at us, thus hindering other people's progress in the process.

Being honest with yourself, no matter the situation, it is

the only way to cut out the deception that you see or hear around you. This, therefore, calls for self-discipline and evaluation of how we relate with the people around us, to avoid spreading information that may not even be true in the first place.

Power and status are the principal factors that can cause people to endorse a false reality. When we have both, either by what we have accomplished, or who we know, we are most likely to hold influence, negative or positive, over the people in our sphere. When some folks choose to tell a lie, it is usually because of the control that the people they consider very powerful have over them.

When you control people's lives, and you have what they want, they will endorse anything you do, whether they agree with it or not. This type of lie is destructive. The people make you feel like you are the greatest person in the world, when in fact they know you are not.

This level of dysfunction is co-dependent; it requires an individual who is incapable of honestly self-assessing and a group of people willing to endorse that lie for a variety of reasons. The main reason for this is that the 'yes men and women' are often fearful of falling out of favour with the 'emperor', and also fear consequences that may come with that.

Sadly, the 'emperor' walking around butt naked is a common sight in many institutions. I speak figuratively and not literally here, thank goodness! When you lie to someone, for whatever reason; you then have to remember what it was you said in the first instance, to ensure that when the same person comes back to you in a similar setting, you stick to your original lie.

But it doesn't end there; you may also need to keep adding to your lie, and to a false narrative to prove to the person you are deceiving that you are on his or her side!

At this point, you have a problem on your hands because you have three different lies making the rounds. In the end, everybody is forced into strengthening a position built on fantasy, all because no one wants to tell the leader the truth, and it becomes a mess.

Lying is exhausting; it lacks integrity and destroys not only the one you are lying to; it destroys you too. Remember, the bible says: *"the truth will set you free"*. I emphasise this because if you tell the truth, you will not be rehearsing trying to remember it. There's an old saying, *"Oh, what a tangled web we weave when first we practice deceiving."*

Why can't I see myself?

Every one of us has a blind spot, that area of our lives that is unseen to us but is quite obvious to others. Without self-awareness, we pass through relationships and life experiences unaware of how others perceive us, and unable to take full responsibility for our shortcomings.

At times, we think that experienced leaders and others in high positions have a greater sense of self-awareness and yet surprisingly; sometimes the opposite is true.

Blind spots can be the Achilles heel of leadership. But

then, weaknesses are simply aspects of our lives that can be strengthened with practice, time, or desire.

These are personal traits or aspects we don't even know we have, but that may limit the way we act, react, behave or believe, thus stifling our personal development in the process.

Insecure people are not the only ones who do not like to hear the truth about them. More often than not, even the ones we think are very confident and successful do not want to know either.

Egotistical leaders, for example, may make it clear from the way they act that they don't want to hear bad news about their organisation. It is even worse when the people who are supposed to speak the truth are afraid to do so, when they can see that things are not going well. Instead, they remain mute, or worst of all, lie.

If we fail to deal with our blind spots, we are in danger of walking around in our imaginary clothes! The only way to effectively deal with our "BS" (blind spots) is to surround ourselves with people who are candid enough to help us become better people.

For me, rightly or wrongly, I thought by asking my leaders to improve in a certain area that I was concerned about, I would be helping to grow our community better. But, as I said earlier, all hell broke loose instead. I learnt something from this situation; I had an epiphany: when a leader's 'entitlement' increases, gratitude or grace always decreases - for those in their inner circle, and for the rest of the people they lead.

I was spoken to, that day, in a way that I had never been, in all my life. What followed was a separation from the people I had considered family for nearly two decades. People had to pick sides, it didn't have to be said, the writing was on the wall, and it was in the air, deeply woven in the fabric of the establishment. Others had already left and were treated the same way, so this response was not surprising, but as in all unhealthy relationships we find ourselves in, we always think, "that cannot happen to me".

It was and still is hard to understand how suggesting action changes could be seen as an attack even when it was done respectfully, although I am sure they would beg to differ on this one.

I learnt, from this incident in particular that our circle of trust must reflect a variety of perspectives, experiences, and approaches to problem-solving to help us adjust and progress in life.

Being able to deal with blind spots helps us, leaders, to create an environment in which people are comfortable to speak the truth. Nothing else demonstrates authentic and mature leadership than the ability to take criticism on the chin.

Wired for truth

As spiritual beings, we are hard-wired for honesty. We have a natural instinct to search for answers and make sense of things. Take acting, for example, it is easy to spot terrible acting on-screen even if you are not an actor yourself.

This is because we are viscerally connected to openness, on a physical and spiritual level. It is part of who we are, and we instinctively reject dishonesty, the same way we do, a virus.

The consequence of overriding this natural impulse by telling lies is the immense amounts of resistance and negative energy generated in our bodies. This internal stress puts us at war with ourselves, as a result causing damage to the very root of the moral fabric that makes us human. So how can we find freedom from the lies we tell others and most importantly, ourselves?

How do we rid ourselves of these limiting beliefs, which is what lies are? We can begin by facing the truth from our experiences and then approach them with the raw honesty and emotion that we have avoided for decades.

Clearing out our emotional closet can be terrifying, but once we have done it, we receive our healing, we change, and we come into maturity as humans. Also, being true to who we are, allows us to maintain a high level of integrity, and peace of mind. Therefore, embrace a life that is guided by values and make decisions based on the truth.

I can't be wrong

King Saul was technically Israel's first king (1 Samuel 8: 4-5). He ascended to the throne after a bloody and turbulent period in Israel's history, under the reign of a diversity of tribal chieftains, called "Judges". The people cried out for a king, but what was he going to be like?

Well, Saul was the kind of king the people deserved – an egocentric, who loved the people's accolades and keeping up appearances, more than the fear of God.

Saul was so deeply flawed that the entire first half of the book of Samuel is dedicated to a character study about his failures.

Actually, his main character flaw was self-exaltation and self-deception. He was a man who thought he knew better than everyone else, God included. And to make matters worse, he was not even aware of it. We can see from the biblical narrative that King Saul was completely blind to his arrogance and always believed that he was in the right.

This is a man who did not know, or possibly did not care to say, "I am sorry" or "I am wrong" (see 1 Samuel 13, 1 Samuel 15). Saul never owned any of his mistakes! He blamed "the people" (1 Samuel 15:15) instead.

But Saul's failures are close to home, at least if we are honest with ourselves. Saul craved the opinion of the people over God's. And so, his arrogance and the people's opinion became the basis for his downfall.

He also loved reputation and honour; these were the two things that were very important to him, from the beginning of his reign, till the end, when a demon began to torment him.

Even then, Saul downplayed his role in the bad decisions he made. He was still bringing in other people as if they were responsible for his mistakes.

Saul's account in the bible should, however, lend us an opportunity for self-reflection to find the blind-spots where our pride may be getting the best of us. Otherwise, we will continue to justify our mistakes until there is nothing else left to justify.

And remember some people are like soldiers of fortune, they will always gravitate towards the person who pays handsomely. They will fight for you today and abandon you when they realise you have nothing more to give to them.
So, do not be fooled by people's praise, support, or false submission. Find your blind spots!

“ You will never
achieve in life,
locked up in the
tomb of people's
negative words.

NOTES:

Who are the leaders in your life that speak into you? Are these people *Lids or Coverings?*

6

THE LID HAS A SOUND

The words from our mouths can have a negative or positive effect on our own lives or the lives of others. I went through a tough year in which words coming from the people I had loved for decades injured me in more ways than I could imagine, for quite a long time. I discovered during that time how emotional pain can drain you of the ability to rationalise things. You fail to see the point as to why people would say things about you that are so hurtful and untrue.

My line of thinking at that time was: In spite of what I may have done to these people, do they feel justified in treating my family and me in a way that they have? I learned how easy it is to lose one's uniqueness and identity, and how failing to manage emotional pain can stop one from transitioning into the next season of their life.

In my case, I sat back to trace the origin of my emotional wounds; I could only trace them back to the words that these people were speaking over my life. In life, you will learn, if you haven't already, that people will applaud you, for as long as you stay exactly where they place you. The moment you decide to reposition yourself, in search of new ground, all hell breaks loose! Have you noticed how when you are about to break into new territory, a storm comes to try to stop you from getting there?

My reasoning is very simple: The words that we allow into our souls carry a 'sound'. That sound can be a progress blocker or a springboard for us to reach new heights in our lives.

The words that become progress blockers in our lives first come from an external source, and then they filter onto the inside to become a sound stuck on repeat mode. Subsequently, we start to say things like, "I will never amount to anything. I am not worth anything, I will never be loved", and the more the recording plays, the tighter the Lid gets on the Container created by those same words.

You better recognise

There was a time when we knew people's names or what

their faces looked like while their thoughts on any given issue remained unknown. And then came social media; the era of instant communication in which opinions have become like buses. You miss one, just keep scrolling; you will surely catch another.

It is important to mention here that I am not knocking social media. I'm an avid user myself. I am merely pointing out how noisy our world has become, and if we are not careful, we are in danger of losing ourselves to its sound.

A Lid as previously defined comes in many guises: things, people, relationships, experiences, and anything that stops you from becoming who you are by their existence in your life.

As I grow older, I am not only paying attention to what people say but more so how they act. I have come to understand that what they say is just noise but what they do? That is intent.

It is a strategy on how to systematically strip you of your confidence and consequently limit your chances at success. As I continued listening, it became increasingly clear that the Lid always announces itself; it is your job to recognise it and respond accordingly.

I have also come to realise that a Lid will:

- Clap for you in private but never ever acknowledge you in public.

- Call you their bestie when it serves their interests but behave differently in the company of people they think are better than you.

- Flatter you with words when you are alone with them but turn around and say something completely different behind your back, to other people.

- Behind your back they speak lies about you, to the people they think are very important, to sabotage your future.

Do you have such a person in your life? The person is without doubt, a Lid. Such people don't mind you helping them, but when it is the other way round; the whole world gets to hear about it. They do this to demean you in the eyes of the people close to you, and society at large. The way someone treats you speaks volumes about him or her. All too often people will put labels on you but only because they have deep-seated insecurities. However, it is your job to try to pick up the sound that precedes their actions.

After what happened to me, I often felt as though my whole world had been ripped from under my feet each time I thought about it. That is because I loved the people and the decision to leave, that place didn't come lightly. Some people may say, well, you started the whole thing you should have just kept silent, but I say no, I ended it! And my point is this: When God starts to shift you in another direction; the last thing you should worry about is people's misconceptions of you, you have to be courageous to end the season in order to embark on the next.

Let God's leading and empowerment take precedence instead. And be careful not to place yourself under leaders who only mentor or pastor you for their gain. I am always of the view that healthy relationships and functional leadership are vital to one's development. However, we must test the culture of an institution to ensure it allows one the freedom to operate according to the prompting of the Holy Spirit and not man's.

Protect that space

Another thing I learnt in my season of what I will call "persecution" is that some words were not necessarily directed at me; they were spoken to determine, or shall I say shrink the boundaries of my territory. However, I realised that the longer I let those words marinate within me, the more I was becoming incapable of getting up and taking the next step towards my destiny.

I let go of the disappointment and shifted my focus from the pain and the hurt of those words. I realised that there was something more to this fight, beyond the experience itself. I mean, who, in his or her right mind fights something, unless it is a threat? The people who fought against me; whether they were conscious of it or not, probably recognised the destiny on my life otherwise, why fight me as they did?

It dawned on me, again, that this war of words was a strategy to stop me from making progress towards my life's dreams and aspirations. The war was about my destiny, my purpose and about all the people that I would later influence. Once I got that, I was able to see clearly, making sense of the storm and my pain. I also came across a passage in scripture that I had read many times before, but which now became so real to me.

The passage is about David and his men coming back from war (1 Samuel 30) only to find that the Amalekites had raided Ziklag, burned it and taken their women as captives.

David came to an empty abode with no clue where his family and livestock were. It must have felt, to David, as though everything was lost and there was no one in Israel to whom he could turn for support.

But at least he had his friends around him, right? Not really. The passage mentioned above says that the people thought of stoning David. No doubt, all the support structures around him were gone and all he had left was his God. So, you would think that David felt as low as anyone could be. However, the bible says:

"But David strengthened himself in the Lord his God" 1 Samuel 30:6, (NKJV).

A lot had happened to bring David to this place, but now he was here - God was his only source of strength.

The lesson here is simple: No matter the situation, maintain a close relationship with the Lord just as David did. The Bible says, *"those who know their God will be strong and they will do exploits,"* no matter how terrible the circumstances are." Daniel 11:32, (NKJV).

Get out!

"The tongue has no bone, but it is strong enough to break a heart", so the saying goes. In my situation, I learnt that the words of the people who were against me would have been a container to constrain me if I would have let them. You will never achieve in life, locked up in the tomb of people's negative words. And you can never fulfil God's call for your life, dwelling on other people's opinions of you.

Divisive and hateful words are as lethal as any murder weapon. Harsh words are indicative of a deeper heart problem. Mostly people who bring others down do it to make themselves feel like they are in control or more powerful or to cover up their own insecurities.

Remember, more often than not when hate lies pulling people down for them is a defence mechanism, because they do not know how to deal with their insecurities. Also, when vitriol is directed at you, the core issue is less likely about you and more about them. It is worth noting, however, to always place the blame externally without doing a bit of introspection.

The responsibility to initiate
change lies within us.

NOTES:

Stay still and listen carefully, what are the words being spoken over you?

7

WHEN IT BECOMES A FRIEND

It is virtually impossible for me to talk about the Lids in my life without telling them through the lens of a black woman. In exploring this further, I found that my experience is one that countless black people face especially in the "Western world." Let's talk about the difficult topic of worshiping whilst black, in white led congregations. It is important for me to state here that however important I believe a leadership must be a reflection of the people they are leading, I am open to being led totally by white leaders if the spirit by which those leaders are chosen is through a system that is fair and spirit led.

For God shows no partiality, Romans 2:11.

As I previously identified, it is very common to see church promotional materials intentionally filled with diverse people to create what I will call an illusion of integration. In reflecting what I had gone through, I learnt that what people of colour are looking for is not just diversity, but rather an innate desire for inclusion. Diversity is a "display" of all people alongside each other whereas Inclusion is the actual merging of people who look like me and accepting that my outlook to life may differ from my white brothers and sisters because of the difference in our experience.

In general, whiteness of the congregation is not something I dwelt on. I developed a relationship with many white people to a level of family, I loved and still love them. However, talking about race is hard, most white people I have come across are not racist; what I am faced with mostly, however, is defensiveness and dismissiveness when the topic of race is raised. The biggest struggle with some of my white friends in my observation, is the failure to see the privileges that come to them just by being born in their skin colour.

So for example, there was a season of terrorist bombings across the west; we stood on the pulpit and made time to pray for Paris, we prayed for Belgium, we even prayed for Australia where there was an attempted attack. Absolutely right call by the way. But, at the same time an African terrorist kidnaps over 1000 girl children and I heard nothing on the pulpit.

A young black boy is gunned down by the police for wearing a hoodie, and still nothing is raised. I tried to raise it with leaders, but they had no idea it had even happened. In my mind the questions began to rise, "we call ourselves family, but I can't sleep over this and it's not even on your radar?"

I honestly do not recall in my time there where my leaders stood up and spoke on issues that were affecting my community, the imbalance was stark. I am unsure what it was, whether it was, ignorance, denial or just a disregard for the things that were breaking a large section of their community.

But we adapt

In a fascinating 19th century science experiment, researchers found that when they put a frog in a pan of boiling water, the frog quickly jumped out. But, when they put the frog in cold water and put the water to boil over time, the frog boiled to death. The hypothesis is that the change in temperature is so gradual, the frog does not realise it's boiling to death. While the results of the experiment are in question it is a good metaphor for organisation cultures" (Inam, Forbes: Leadership and the boiling frog experiment, 2013).

This illustration reminds me of my previous experiences with the leaders at my old church. Sometimes we listen to conversations that make us uncomfortable but like the frog we have slowly adapted and somewhat become numb to the things we should be standing up and saying "NO, this is not ok."

I think it is important that the church begins to have the difficult conversations about race. White folk need to be open to listen and understand that when black people talk about race, they are merely looking for a space with family where they feel heard. For black people, we need to gather courage to speak and not suffer in silence in a place that is supposed to be home.

It is important for us to be honest about how we are feeling by overcoming the fear of being ostracised for speaking up. Adapting to discomfort does not grow or change the environment as the "frog water" continues to grow hotter and eventually the very essence of who you are dies.

Is anything even wrong?

Sometimes you will find that the most difficult thing to do is getting people to just acknowledge the obvious. As a minority you experience verbal and nonverbal rebuffs on a constant basis, the sad reality is we have grown to adapt and excuse it. What is difficult to stomach however is when these attacks come from people whom we believe should be standing with us. This behaviour is overt in the world but hidden in the churches so we may be forgiven in thinking that it is not there.

Look around you, when you find black majority churches run by white leaders you will find more often a lack of representation of black leadership in the rooms of power.

Too often as black people we have avoided talking about the feeling of a lack of true representation for fear of being labelled as divisive. When black people speak up about our experiences, there is an expectation on us to prove beyond reasonable doubt that how we felt about an incident was valid!

Many white people wrongly assume that racism only includes overt acts, such as calling someone the 'n-word' or expressly excluding black people from groups or organisations. This is limited in thinking because what is more dangerous and common is a muted response in the face of injustice or uncritical support of the status quo by silence. When we are silent, we are part of the problem and are well and truly complicit. I have found that the pain of the racial issues we face at times pales in comparison to the indifference we see with the white leadership in the church.

Level playing field

The greatest misconception is assuming that black and white people start from a level playing field when it comes to opportunities in churches. This has not been my experience, the weirder your name (well, weird to them), the thicker your accent and darker your skin tone, the less likely you were to be offered any leadership role regardless of how obvious your leadership calling was.

There is often language of making sure we build church "culture." What I learnt was church culture is a code word for "our" culture. We talk about the church being multicultural but what we actually mean is that the church is multi-racial. Unless you look, speak and dress like us there is no hope for you. I learnt to adapt but adapting meant suppressing the core of who I was, I knew there were elements of myself I couldn't bring to the table because it threatened who they were.

I also got tired of hearing conversations between black people, discussing how they felt about "worshiping whilst black" but then at the same time putting their "game face" on in front of the white leaders they had been talking about. It was this inability to stand up against what they saw as an unfair system that I believe preserved the problems. I was in that place for nearly two decades and believe I contributed a lot of good. I too, however, must have been part of the problem perpetuating a system that was stunting personal growth of people who looked like me.

As much as I had white family in the church, it was painfully evident to me that I was in an environment that had a shortage of awareness and hence empathy for issues of racial inequality. This led to the black people standing passively in the face of inequality and injustice. How can we change anything by standing on the side-lines, talking about it in our own groups but frightened to challenge the face of it? The answer I found was an unvoiced fear among black people in the church to speak up for fear of being labelled rebellious and thus curtailing any chances of leadership opportunities.

But we can change, it will take black people with access to leadership and influence, to cast aside all discomfort, put their necks on the line and speak for the majority who are not in that position. It is not just enough to post outrage on social media, at what we see as overt racism and yet not do anything about the day to day decisions we are making as leaders that are slowly killing the essence of the people in the very community you are trying to build. For me, because of the access and what I thought was a bridge of relationship with leadership, I stood up to make a stand at some of the uncomfortable practices I was seeing. Unfortunately, it didn't work for me as my relationship with the leaders had sadly broken down.

Just because it didn't work for me, however, doesn't mean it is not an approach to take. There has to be more and more black people with voice, influence and church standing that put themselves in the line of fire. I am not asking for people to become spokespeople for their race, but rather I am asking that it becomes all our responsibility to educate ourselves of issues that affect us and be prepared to stand up and speak on them when required.

A unified approach?

It remains my firm belief that change will have to come from the church in order to tackle this inequality. The test is if we are committed to seeing a diverse world then we need to be unified in taking responsibility for each other. It is important to understand that not all white people are naïve about race and not all black people are "woke." Someone has to stick their head above the parapet and shout "this is not ok!"

There are plenty of examples in the bible that show how communities stood up to fight against oppression. Let's take Esther for example. She heard what was happening to her people. Even though she was in a position of privilege she risked all she had to go and stand before the king unannounced, in order to speak for her people.

Esther 4: 12-14, (NIV).

When Esther's words were reported to Mordecai, he sent back this answer: "Do not think that because you are in the king's house you alone of all the Jews will escape. For if you remain silent at this time, relief and deliverance for the Jews will arise from another place, but you and your father's family will perish. And who knows but that you have come to your royal position for such a time as this?"

It had been about five years since the wedding, and it appears the honeymoon may have been over for Esther. Approaching the King was a risk to even her life! Sometimes doing the right thing requires a risky step of faith. In order to change what is necessary in the environment we find ourselves we will need to, like Esther, put our fear aside and risk all to speak up for what is right. In the end however, God is sovereign and will accomplish his program with or without us.

Soul searches

My experiences made me grow as a person. I have healed and let go of many hurts. The greatest lesson I learnt in my church experience is that passivity in the face of an unjust system never changed it. If I could do it all over again, I would hope that I would gather enough courage to speak up sooner.

I wish I had confronted things much earlier when questions began to form in my mind. But hindsight is a wonderful thing, and I am sure those who know me will read this thinking, "Why didn't you get out?"

Well, the answer is simple. I loved these people, and as a result I trusted them. Where there is trust, it takes a lot for one to stand up and go against the grain.

Speaking up came at a price, for me, life became unbearable and forced me to make the decision to leave. I realise now, how easy it is for people to allow circumstances to continue because of fear of what we see as powerful forces. Those unaffected may think that whatever is happening does not really concern them when in fact it does; After all, we are our 'brother's keepers'.

Biblical frogs

The responsibility to initiate change lies with us. Nothing changes until we decide it must. I am, therefore, reminded of Pharaoh's encounter with Moses, in the book of Exodus. The Israelites had been in Bondage, in Egypt, for over four hundred years. Moses, acting on God's command, approached Pharaoh asking for the Israelites to be set free. Exodus 5:1 says:

Afterward Moses and Aaron went and said to Pharaoh, "Thus says the LORD, the God of Israel, 'Let my people go, that they may hold a feast to me in the wilderness.'"

But Pharaoh stubbornly refused to grant the request. So, God sent plagues upon Egypt to pressure him to release his people.

God released ten plagues upon Egypt, and one of them involved frogs covering the part of the country occupied by the Egyptians.

There were frogs everywhere. Frogs in the water, frogs in the fields, frogs in their homes, and I suppose in their pots and beds. It was at this point that Moses approached Pharaoh explaining that if he let his people go, he would pray for the frogs to go. Pharaoh's answer is mind-blowing!

Exodus 8:8-10, (NIV)

"Pharaoh summoned Moses and Aaron and said, "Pray to the Lord to take the frogs away from me and my people, and I will let your people go to offer sacrifices to the Lord. Moses said to Pharaoh, "I leave to you the honour of setting the time for me to pray for you and your officials and your people that you and your houses may be rid of the frogs, except for those that remain in the Nile." Tomorrow," Pharaoh said.

Tomorrow?

What in the world possessed Pharaoh to ask for one more night with the frogs? I think it is the fear, among other things, of what he realised was going to be a life-changing decision.

But as the saying goes, *"Denial is not just a river in Egypt"*. Pharaoh is not the only one willing to spend one more night with the frogs. Many of us tolerate many exasperating situations in our lives simply because we are afraid of change. We need to let go of the "frog" because every time we say "tomorrow", we delay stepping into our God-given destiny.

"

God is sovereign and will accomplish
His programme with or without us.

NOTES:

What habits can you identify that have been holding you back? What are you going to do to get rid of them?

8

WHEN THE UNACCEPTABLE IS UNACCEPTABLE

A lot has so far been said about various types of "Lids" in this book, but the question still remains: What makes people tolerate situations that they know are toxic to their personal development and wellbeing?

Much like the discussion about Pharaoh and the frogs in the previous chapter, I would like us to unpack the *'why'* of the issue.

Why do we as humans often allow hurtful events, people, and processes to repeatedly torment our lives?

I found for me, for example, that I tolerated toxic leaders and friends because at that time I may have had a distorted internal (and to an extent, external) image of myself, making me feel weak, and unsure of who I was and the confidence that I was of any true worth.

There are events, people and processes whose existence we have at times allowed to continue in our lives; a toxic leader, a friend who we know behaves terribly or even a dysfunctional relationship, the list is endless. In my observation, there are overarching reasons we tolerate behaviours which leave us bound in insecurity and low self-worth.

Am I who they say I am?

Sadly, as humans, we at times keep ourselves small and powerless, and allow external and to an extent, internal, dialogue to shrink our confidence. We question our talents and experiences, and in the process, we get paralysed with doubt and feelings of worthlessness.

Thinking about my own journey as I have outlined in this book so far, I realise that I had to a certain extent, tolerated the Lid of dysfunction. But this boiled down primarily to foundational issues linked to my past.

Say, for example, if one had emotionally manipulative or narcissistic people around them in their childhood years, they are most likely to struggle in the area of building appropriate boundaries that allow them to say "NO!" to behaviour that is violating, manipulative and oppressive.

If it's unacceptable to you...

If this sounds familiar to you, then it is time to start "finding brave" and begin the process of knowing yourself intimately and honouring what you believe, and feel is right.

I believe a large proportion of people can recognise and understand that the behaviour they observe around and against them, in any given environment, is wrong and should not be tolerated.

In some instances, I failed to muster the strength to say or do anything about situations I considered unacceptable. In the end, I endorsed dysfunctional behaviour, under a misguided notion that things would change.

Monkey say monkey do

The subtle coercion from the people in leadership, to keep you silent on issues that are clearly dysfunctional corrodes who you are, to a point where you begin to believe the lie that is put before you.

It took everything within me to initially start setting limits. This is the area where most people sell themselves short. We feel because we have a relationship with someone at some level, that we have no way to control the *chaos*. This couldn't be further from the truth. Once you find a way to rise above an individual, you begin to find their behaviour more predictable and easier to understand. This equips you to think rationally about when you have to put up with them and when you don't.

I once read somewhere, that when you begin to set boundaries about what is acceptable or not in your life, those people who have been taking advantage of you will begin to call you difficult.

This is so true. It is my firm belief that it is easier to label one's boundaries as difficult, than to look at ourselves and maybe challenge our own behaviours in those areas.

So here I was, accused of not being grateful, for the kindness, which, according to them, had been afforded to me. Side note: I believe we cannot treat people in a certain way, and at the same time determine by our measure, how they should feel about the kind of treatment they have just received. *Let me be the one that tells you how good you treated me!*

Never shy away from taking control of a chaotic situation because you think someone has connections in high places. Once I stood up against a system, I was labelled difficult and lies spread about me that were difficult to refute as the people spreading them were the people in power so to speak. I looked up to these people. I respected them; it was shocking to me how they could lie with impunity and from my perspective get away with it.

However, I learned a lesson in this season, and it was that it was okay for people not to know my side of the story. My grandmother used to say, the truth is like a pregnancy, it is bound to show up one day!

Live to fight another day

Successful people know how important it is to live to fight another day, especially when your foe is a "toxic" individual. I am considered a passionate person, if something is not right in my view; you are going to know about it one way or the other. I am learning however, that in conflict, unchecked emotions make you dig your heels in and fight the kind of battle that can leave you severely damaged.

If you can read and respond to your emotions, you are then able to choose your battles wisely and only stand your ground when the time is right.

People exhibiting Lid tendencies will drive you crazy because their behaviour, whether they recognise it or not, is extremely irrational. Make no mistake about it; their behaviour truly goes against reason. So why allow yourself to respond to them emotionally and get sucked into the mix?

I learnt that the more irrational and off-base someone is, the easier it should be for you to remove yourself from their trap. Quit trying to beat them at their own game. You don't need to respond to the emotional chaos—only the facts.

Maintaining an emotional distance requires awareness. You can't stop someone from pushing your buttons if you don't recognise when that behaviour is happening. Sometimes you'll find yourself in situations where you'll need to refocus and choose the best way forward. This is fine and you shouldn't be afraid to buy yourself some time to do so.

Don't let it steal your joy

When your sense of pleasure and satisfaction are derived

from the opinions of other people, you are no longer the master of your own happiness. When emotionally intelligent people feel good about something that they've done, they won't let anyone's opinions or snide remarks take that away from them.

While it's impossible to turn off your reactions to what others do to you, you don't have to compare yourself to them, and you can always take people's opinions with a grain of salt. That way, no matter what they are thinking or doing, your self-worth comes from within. Also, regardless of what people think of you at any particular moment, one thing is certain—you're never as good or bad as they say you are. Therefore, I believe it is our moral obligation to speak up where injustice prevails.

First they Came

I think that the following excerpt best illustrates the point I just raised above:

German philosopher Martin Niemöller was born in the Westphalian town of Lippstadt, Germany, in the 1800's.

Niemöller enjoyed a successful military and political career. A political turning point in Niemöller's political sympathies came with a meeting of Adolf Hitler. Niemöller and two prominent Protestant bishops met to discuss state pressures on churches. At the meeting it became clear that Niemöller's phone had been tapped by the German Secret State Police. It was also clear that the Pastors Emergency League (PEL), which Niemöller had helped found, was under close state surveillance. Following the meeting, Niemöller would come to see the

Nazi state as a dictatorship, one which he would oppose.

Niemöller is perhaps best remembered for the following quotation:

"First, they came for the socialists, and I did not speak out—because I was not a socialist

Then they came for the trade unionists, and I did not speak out— because I was not a trade unionist,

Then they came for the Jews, and I did not speak out-because I was not a Jew,

And then they came for me- and there was no one left to speak for me"

(The holocaust encyclopedia).

In other words, Martin was saying that the Germans, who kept quiet while millions of innocent people were persecuted and murdered, were just as guilty as the people who had committed these murders in the first place. Silence can cost lives, jobs, families, and even whole communities. It is for this reason that I have always refused to turn a blind eye to acts of injustice. It does not have to happen to you for you to speak up, just because it's not happening to you doesn't make you less responsible for speaking up.

Don't try to bury issues, and don't pretend you are very strong. It is important to listen to what your heart is telling you and deal with it. Otherwise, you are sitting on a ticking emotional time bomb.

"
Honour what
you believe.

NOTES:

Is the environment you are in aiding or hindering your growth? What negative issues have you allowed to linger? How do you think you can get rid of them?

9

NO RANKS TO CLIMB

In one moment, all my relationships changed. Our stability as a family, as we previously knew it, was gone. Most people who had professed their love for us; people we had supported emotionally and financially, people we had welcomed into our home and had dined with us, all turned their backs on us. All this happened because of the decision I took at the time; to speak out against a wrong that had been happening.

It felt like we lost almost 20 years of our lives. My girls lost a sense of belonging and a circle of people and friends they had known all their lives. I penned one letter, and everything changed! No attempt to adequately understand where I was coming from or even a genuine attempt to ask me to stay. What I got in response to my challenge to do better, was instead anger, not sadness, not confusion, but raw plain anger.

This reaction stunned me to the core. I had never, in all my life, been spoken to, in the manner that the leader in this church had spoken to me. I am someone's wife and a mother for goodness sake. Besides, I had authority over others in my sphere of influence and never in a million years would I speak to them in the way he spoke to me. It took us many months to feel normal again and to establish new relationships that we could say we trusted.

We needed a year of therapy after doubting ourselves, feeling sad and lost. My girls have their own story to tell. We kept hearing false information coming from people who we thought could have behaved differently. We saw manipulation and downright untrue and nasty at best from people "of the cloth".

I did not bother asking myself how these people could perpetrate such lies to manipulate others because they will have to answer to God for that. What I grappled with the most was the people around them, who saw and understood that my intent was not malicious, but still endorsed this behaviour and refused to stand up and speak truth.

How could these people who promised to love us suddenly turn their backs on us? It dawned on me that the relationships that I thought were unconditional were conditional, only when the leadership were accepting of me.

It became clear that they wanted people to pick a side, to prove their allegiance. It could be their assessment of me was that I was of no significance or benefit to them and was thus easy to discard. I eventually found peace in that too.

No ranks?

I had seen it happening to other people when I was in that organisation. It's funny when you see it happening to other people; you somehow think it can never happen to you. I saw this same behaviour towards other leaders who chose to leave. The lies, the manipulations, the snide remarks, the cycle of hate, the list is endless, all this in a church!

In retrospect, my story is now easy to tell, because I speak from a position of strength and not judgement. It's a story that's necessary to recount. It's not an attack on any organisation; it's not a spiritual attack, but rather, it's an *"alarm"*, to say let's behave differently when we know better.

The sooner we realise and accept that life is not a ladder to be climbed for people's approval, the sooner we begin to grow. Personal growth happens when we free ourselves from always wanting to please people. How can we bring out the rich and authentic versions of who we are if we always have to filter ourselves through other people's expectations of us?

In my case, I grew in strength and experienced first-hand the meaning of the phrase, "what doesn't kill you makes you stronger". You cannot give up just because your world has been turned upside down, stand your ground and get it back to how it is supposed to be or even better! If losing the people who could so easily replace me, is what I needed to be on the right side of the truth, then I would speak up again if necessary. I refuse to lose my self-respect for a position.

Remember there are no ranks to climb; you have a unique voice and race. Park yourself and pause, if you need to, but keep going and speak up, when you need to, and never allow yourself to be silenced.

Don't doubt yourself

Lids can make you doubt yourself, wrap your destiny up, and go home! When I was writing, 'All Grown Up', my debut book, I was very excited. I have always had a way with words, and a lot of people had suggested I write a book. I had tried blogging and had enjoyed a level of success with my 'Life with Leah' social media pages, but still, I did not think I could write a book.

I was pregnant with this book for years before birthing it. Why? Because self-doubt can delay legitimate destiny! When I finally set about writing my manuscript, a bit like a stab in the dark, I produced reams of words. In my mind, the story was taking shape.

When I finished, I got in touch with an editor to discuss how I could get my words on paper, to a publisher. After first overcoming my self-doubt to finally write the book, you can imagine my shock when the editor I had approached came back to me with the following response (I have changed names and paraphrased to protect those involved):

> *"Hi Leah,*
> *After reading through what I've got so far, I took the first two paragraphs of chapter 1 and thought they have potential for a prologue/introduction to the book. I've duly made comments on the side, and as you'll see, because of virtually repetition, there is very little left of the original text. I can imagine to a new writer such a 'hacking down' could be somewhat disheartening, but hopefully it will enable you to focus your thoughts better.*
>
> *Having looked at the chapters for a start, I think it needs to be scrapped and she needs to start again.*
>
> *All for now, blessings".*

Are you kidding me? What did they mean my book needed "throwing away?" Did they even know how long it had taken me to gather courage to put my thoughts down on paper?

It is important to note that these people may have had the best intention for me and my writing ambition, but the delivery of what they were saying had the potential to become a Lid in my life. It is also key to recognise a Lid when you encounter one, because in this instance what I was essentially hearing was someone telling me, can my dreams...If I dared!

This was a defining moment to me as a potential writer, I knew I could write, internally, I believed I had the words to make it. But here I was facing a panel of experts, these were potentially the obstacles between me and my future ambition to be an author. I had a choice to give up and be subsumed by emotions of failure or ignore them and continue, I chose the latter.

In the bible, David encountered a similar obstacle on his way to becoming king, in Israel.

We read in I Samuel 17:28, (NIV):

When Eliab, David's oldest brother, heard him speaking with the men, he burned with anger at him and asked, "Why have you come down here? And with whom did you leave those few sheep in the wilderness? I know how conceited you are and how wicked your heart is; you came down only to watch the battle.

David's oldest brother was annoyed because to him, David was just a shepherd boy. But "Hey, Eliab this is your future king, buddy"!

To realise your dream, you need to go beyond the Lid. You must stand up to your mountains and do something about them. David did exactly that. He did not let this encounter with his brother slow him down or even stop him. It is clear to me that David had the throne in mind!

When you have a mind-set of an overcomer, no one's experience, or seniority can intimidate you. You will find that the mountains that make you fearful, in your mind, don't even possess half the strength you think they have over you.

A Lid can immobilise and limit you if you permit it, but

you can change that today. If you run into a wall, it's not time to turn around and give up. Figure out how to climb over it, go through it, or work around it, if you must.

After reading the initial review from the panel of expert editors I mentioned earlier, I peeled myself off the floor, picked up my pen and continued to write.
Every editor is useful; none of them are "bad". Some are annoying, so much that you want to drop-kick them into a moat full of unpleasant things.

However, a good writer overlooks the irritation and digs down to the issues. I feel the need to say here, that I have found an editor who gets me. He has a way of helping with my manuscripts without me feeling like an absolute failure!

Where did that come from?

I once read an excerpt that said, "A calm mind is an ultimate weapon to the challenges we encounter". How fascinating is that? My mind used to run at 100 miles an hour until some form of external trauma forced me to stop!
Just because something negative was said about you; it does not mean you have to adopt it as truth. I have learnt that we must never take any thoughts attached to a traumatic experience seriously. Show fortitude in the face of the perpetrators, and you will sooner or later prove them wrong.

The final Lid

While this book is based on personal experience, it still has done two things for me: It has given me the space to stand in who I am and what I believed about myself. It has also helped me to read my bible, to gain inspiration from those who have gone before me, having smashed their Lids.

Even Jesus faced the ultimate lid, Satan's voice taunting him to climb down from the cross if He indeed was the son of God.

Mathew 27:40, (NIV) tells us this,

And saying, "You who are going to destroy the temple and build it in three days, save yourself! Come down from the cross if you are the Son of God"!

Are we not glad some of us are not God? If that was me facing the cross I would have been like, "crucify me? Nope, off the cross I come"! But Jesus recognised this voice as a Lid meant to derail him from his purpose to free mankind.

Behave differently when you
know better.

NOTES:

What areas have you identified that you need to develop in order for you to get to the next level?

10

CALCIFICATION OF THE END

The purpose of this book is to help shed light on the barriers we face in life, and why at times it feels as though we have failed to reach our potential. I call these barriers, Lids, all through this book.

Having reflected on the Lids we have faced in life, there has to be an end in which we have not only cracked those Lids but also ultimately smashed them. The sound of the smash signifies that you have come to the end of one season and are ready to transition into the next.

Our response in every season, therefore, is not only to

draw a line, to mark its end, but to also gather some valuable lessons. Thus, the end of every season entails making drastic changes, some are easy to embrace, while others are not, yet the change still must be made.

Also, reflecting and introspecting are vital to achieving one's goal, regardless of the situation. The following excerpts from my journal best sum up my life's lessons detailed in this book:

- *Never discarded so easily*
- *Never been challenged so deeply*
- *Never saw more clearly*
- *Never been shocked so painfully*
- *Never embraced so freely*
- *But never felt so free...*

I now understand why things happened the way they did, and I understand the reasons behind it all. However, in all of this, I also learnt that merely understanding the reasons does not erase the hurt one has been through.

In the bible, James says:

Consider it pure joy, my brothers, and sisters, whenever you face trials of many kinds, because you know that the testing of your faith produces perseverance. James 1:2, (NIV).

So, consider it a blessing in disguise when people turn against you, because it's in times of crisis that your mind works at its best. Also, the measure of your test determines your credibility. The greatest faith lessons in life are often learned in the dark. God uses trials to develop us spiritually.

Mirror, Mirror

I have been told I am strong headed. Some people say when I take a position on an issue; I stick to it like a dog with a bone. However, experience has taught me that one cannot be right all the time. It is, therefore, good to reflect on one's path in life, to avoid repeating certain mistakes because of not being open to what others have to say.

Reflection helps us chart a better way forward. Sometimes we are too quick to block people's numbers from our phone books, because we are hurt and have moved on. But I guess every person has their way of dealing with issues. For me, it's important that I let go of the words that tried to hold me captive; there is no better way to move forward. So yes, go ahead and block the number sis, if it helps, but clearing the conversation threads? That's a wrap!

After assessing my stand from the past events, I realised I had removed a few people from my phone contacts list but was still holding on to the conversations that were killing me. I am not sure why I was holding on to these texts as they were too painful to reread. But now that I am stronger, I look back, and I find it funny that I was holding on to the conversations as if they were evidence to prove to a fictitious judge in my mind about how cruel some individuals had been to me.

Someone said this to me, and it helped: "deleting the conversation doesn't mean what they did was right, nor does it mean you'll forget, but you'll stop rehearsing it, and over time it will fade away." I say all this to show how you need to push yourself to let stuff go, to give yourself a chance of survival after being hurt.

War wounds

When you have been through life's battles, you may come out bruised, like when one has been in a war; they get wounded. Some of my wounds are from the mistakes I made, and some are because I was living. I call these the war wounds.

The problem, however, is that when we have been wounded in war, we may convince ourselves that we are disqualified from living out God's purpose for our lives. However, such wounds have the power to push us into God's purpose.

God at times reveals our purposes through our wounds. Someone once said this to me and I believe it is true: "there is nothing we go through in life that is ever wasted". David, in the bible, sustained some wounds after he had fought the lion and the bear. However, the wounds didn't disqualify him; they instead empowered him to face the giant, Goliath, on his way to becoming King.

But David persisted. "I have been taking care of my father's sheep and goats," he said. "When a lion or a bear comes to steal a lamb from the flock, I go after it with a club and rescue the lamb from its mouth. If the animal turns on me, I catch it by the jaw and club it to death. I have done this to both lions and bears, and I'll do it to this pagan Philistine, too, for he has defied the armies of the living God!" 1 Samuel 17:34-36, (NLT).

There is an important period in David's life that I think many people know very little about – the time David, as a shepherd-boy, tended his father's flock. David had his adventures and challenges all at the same time. This was the time in which he fought a lion and a bear.

You don't come out of a fight with a bear clean. David must have had some cuts; he must have had a limp of some sort, and yet this fight with the bear didn't stop him from fighting the giant.

This book is meant to help us recognise and overcome the lids we encounter in life. A constant readjustment of our focus is vital to overcoming the "Lids". Also, reflecting on the past seasons of your life and your feelings in that period is very important. I learnt from experience to view difficult times as seasons of personal improvement and creativity. I have learnt that irrespective of the Lids we encounter in life, we will one day look back to those challenging moments as among some of the most formative of our lives.

In the middle of my midnight hour, I wrote this in my journal.

You cannot let a Lid contain you; you cannot let it change the course of your destiny because you became bitter. It is important to look beyond individuals and see yourself in the future. Stop trying to get your side of the story heard; they have made up their mind anyway. A time will come when you will need to speak out; a time when you are speaking from a position of strength. Love and let go of people don't let bitterness blind you of the joy you have around you. Let go of being right and concentrate on where you want to be.

You have to let go of all the hurt that you went through. Look at yourself as a war veteran; someone who has been through battles. And once you decide to let it go, you must let it go. This is a process; it does not change overnight. You must, therefore, be patient with yourself.

The veteran

I think that coming out of a traumatic situation is like a veteran returning home from war. You would think that the greatest challenge for any soldier is having bullets whizzing past him or her. And you would be forgiven for thinking that peace and confidence always follow the end of a "war". However, the outcome is often the opposite, as the difficult patch is after the conflict has ended; when it is time to leave behind the memories of what happened.

Failing to move past hurtful memories and the people who caused the hurt is a waste of valuable time. Besides, rehashing it will keep you from living a meaningful life. As "war veterans"; we can move on from any Lid with dignity, integrity, and love. Nothing we face in life is ever wasted. Every experience, painful or otherwise, is valuable. What we do with it is up to us.

Lessons

I learnt that every lid I faced and fought helped me to birth something. I also learnt how I must critically analyse the situation that I am in and figure out my next step from there.

Be a lifelong learner. Wisdom calls for you to embrace your experiences. Be honest, straightforward and act in integrity always. A wise woman once said to me, "When you conduct yourself honourably, God will always vindicate you."

The further and further away I was, from the Lid situations that caused me pain, the clearer I was able to rationalise things. I saw how some people had clapped for me but only when things worked in their favour. I saw how what I thought was family was premised on me being who they wanted me to be; I found out that what I thought was friendship was not necessarily their definition of how friendship should be; I saw how people who claimed to love me could in a heartbeat look me in the eye as if I never existed; I saw how the people I had poured myself into; those whom I had supported and helped, shut the door on me with such ease because of what they had heard. True or false, it didn't matter.

And finally, I saw the dysfunctional human side of leadership, and this helped me to let go of disappointment as a person. Let the Lids that you encounter in life help you to grow too.

It has been an incredible journey, one that I believe is still unfolding. I must say also that it will take you some time to realise that you really do have freedom now, and it is up to you to learn what to do with it. Whatever it is you do with it, make sure it benefits you. Take as long as you need to rebuild your life, make sure it's on your terms.

" Wisdom calls for you to embrace your experiences.

NOTES:

List the things you need to remove from your life that you identify as having been holding you back.

Epilogue

The process of writing this book helped me to grow as a person. It enabled me to explore aspects of my character that I had never explored before. Smashing Lids is not easy; however, I learnt that any meaningful breakthrough, by its very name, requires something to break. It may not necessarily mean a physical breaking, but it requires an emotional and mental shift into the next level. When we are faced with standing up to mountains, fear must not be an option. We must trust the Lord and act in spite of our fear.

In the season I call "persecution", the Lord gave me this scripture:

The LORD will fight for you; you need only to be still. Exodus 14:14, (NIV).

Though fear made the Israelites want to run from Pharaoh, the Lord told them to stand still; God had their back. We too must choose not to fear, by ensuring we understand that we were called to fulfil our obligations in the challenging situations we encounter. In taking a stand, however, we do not stand alone as we must be assured that the Lord is with us. This scripture makes us fully assured that we are under God's protection and perfect timing.

The reality of all this though, is that it is very hard to believe a scripture can ever come true when days turn to months and months into a year. For me, it felt as though God had promised to vindicate me, but it did not feel like He was doing anything about it.

Making tough decisions should be considered a part of evolving as human beings. Some of the decisions we make may be unpopular, nonetheless if we have examined our situations and deemed the action necessary then my advice is "ride it out", God does come through, He came through for me!

I found comfort in the words of our Lord Jesus Christ in John 16:21, in which He said:

It will be like a woman suffering the pains of labour. When her child is born, her anguish gives way to joy because she has brought a new baby into the world.

I pray this book challenges you to look at the different Lids you have faced or may even still be facing. More importantly I pray that you gather the courage to take the first steps towards change and speak up even when it makes you unpopular.